THERESE

OF LISIEUX

by
Vernon Johnson

*"My longing will be the same
in Heaven as upon earth:
to love Jesus and to make Him loved."
(Thérèse, from a letter to a missionary)*

*All booklets are published thanks to the
generous support of the members of the
Catholic Truth Society*

CATHOLIC TRUTH SOCIETY
PUBLISHERS TO THE HOLY SEE

Contents

In the World **4**

   Home and Infancy 4

   School Days 10

   First Communion 18

   Apostolic Zeal 21

   Forcing the Gates of Carmel 23

   In Rome 29

In Carmel **33**

   Novitiate and Profession 33

   The Saint's Spirituality 41

   Last Illness 51

   Last Months 58

In Heaven **66**

   The Autobiography 67

   The Shower of Roses 68

   A World-Wide Devotion 71

   The Pilgrimage to Lisieux 73

   The Canonisation 74

   Proclaimed Doctor of the Church 82

Epilogue **87**

Acknowledgements

All the quotations in this pamphlet have been taken from the official documents, published by the Carmel through the Office Central of Lisieux. Great use has been made of the official life, *St Thérèse of the Child Jesus*, written by Msgr Leveilla.

Thérèse in the garden at Carmel, 7th June 1897, 3 months before she died.

IN THE WORLD

Home and Infancy

On 2nd January 1873, in a simple house in the rue de Saint Blaise, Alençon, a little child was born whose name was one day to be upon the lips of Catholics the whole world over, and whose prayers and sacrifices were to win souls to God in every corner of the earth. That little child was Marie Françoise Thérèse Martin, later to be raised to the Altars of the Church as St Thérèse of the Child Jesus and of the Holy Face, and to be known more popularly as "the little Flower".

The surroundings of her birth, outwardly at least, gave no indication of the wonderful future that was to follow. Her father, M. Louis Martin, had a small watchmaker's and jeweller's business in the rue du Pont Neuf, and his wife, Zélie Martin, added to the family resources by making and selling Alençon lace. Both M. Martin and his wife were most devout Catholics. Every morning at 5.30 they attended Mass at the Church of Notre Dame, and though daily Communion was not possible they endeavoured to receive the Blessed Sacrament as often as they could. In spite of the fatiguing duties of the household and of the business, they observed the fasts and abstinences of the Church most rigorously, and that at a time when the spirit of mortification among the more comfortably situated families was growing weak. Although Sunday was the favourite day for the country folk to come to Alençon to make their purchases, nothing would induce M. Martin to keep his business open on that day. Along with this sternness in principle there went a great tenderness of heart and a deep compassion for all in suffering or in any kind of misery, which made their house the resort of all who were in any kind of need.

Into this atmosphere of strength and tenderness little Thérèse Martin was born. She was the youngest of nine children. Four of them had died quite young, two of whom were little boys. Their death was a grievous disappointment to the parents, who from the first had always prayed that God would give them among their children one who should be a priest and a saint. Of the remaining four sisters, Marie was the eldest, and to her therefore was entrusted the care of little Thérèse in her earliest years. Quiet and reserved, unwavering in principle but with all the tenderness of a little mother, she laid the first foundations of the character of the future Saint.

Notwithstanding her continual contact with her sister Marie, it was not however this sister who exercised the most marked influence on the character of St Thérèse. Strange to relate it was the example of a sister who at first lived for the most part away at school. This sister was Pauline, the second daughter. Stranger still it was a little word concerning the vocation of Pauline which suggested the destiny of St Thérèse. She tells us this expressly herself. "From the time I commenced to speak, whenever my mother would ask me, 'Of what are you thinking?' my invariable answer was 'of Pauline'. Sometimes I heard them say that Pauline would be a nun, then without knowing too well what it meant I thought to myself, 'I will be a nun, too'. This is one of my first memories. It was her example that from the age of two years drew me towards the Divine Spouse of Virgins." Surely a wonderful message from God to this little soul through that sister who after having unconsciously drawn her towards the cloister from her earliest years was afterwards to be her official guide, as Prioress, in the way of perfection! It was this consciousness of vocation to a life of perfection which explains the heroic resolution of Thérèse at the age of three never to refuse anything to Jesus.

The influence of the third sister, Leonie, was less marked; a delicate and affectionate child, she lavished great tenderness on her baby sister, nursing her and singing her to sleep, but she does not seem to have taken much part in the formation of Thérèse. The last remaining sister, Céline, the next in age to Thérèse, could not have the same influence on account of her tender years. She was however a child of exceptionally sweet and lively disposition, the confidante of her little sister and her constant companion in every childish game. It was Céline more than any other who was to create round little Thérèse that atmosphere of radiant joy, the memory of which made her ever afterwards bless "those sunny years of childhood".

In this home, from the very first, little Thérèse found herself cradled in the supernatural and surrounded by the tenderest human affection. To this she responded with all the power of her affectionate nature. She tells us herself: "My first recollections are of loving smiles and tender caresses: but if God made others love me so much, He made me love them too, for I was of an affectionate nature. You can hardly imagine how much I loved my father and mother and, being very demonstrative, I showed my love in a thousand little ways, though the means I employed make me smile now when I think of them".

This deep affection was not however to be restricted to her family alone. In the midst of the Catholic piety upon which the home was founded and under the example and guidance of her sisters, her immense capacity for loving was directed above all to that Heavenly Father, the God who is the source of all our human loves. It was in this home life that she learnt to seek "to give pleasure to Jesus" in everything she did, and into this she threw herself with all the energy with which she sought to give pleasure to, and to show her love to, her parents and her sisters. Not only was she affectionate but exceedingly frank and direct. Her mother writes: "She has a remarkable intellect and a heart of gold and is absolutely

frank". From the very beginning there was a certain open
directness which was sometimes disconcerting. One day
her sister Leonie, who had outgrown her dolls, brought a
basket of toys to her two little sisters. Céline chose a little
ball. Thérèse, after a moment's pause, put out her hand
and said: 'I choose all!' Later on that trait was to be seen
in her character when, confronted with the call to
perfection and to the making of sacrifices for her Beloved,
she cried: 'I will not be a Saint by halves, I choose all!'

But this strength of purpose and frank directness might
very easily have been a great danger. When she was three
years old we find her mother writing: "Céline is naturally
inclined to be good; as for the little puss Thérèse one cannot
tell how she will turn out, she is so young and heedless, a
very intelligent child but of not nearly so sweet a
disposition as her sister, her stubbornness is almost
unconquerable. When she has said 'No', nothing will make
her change: one could leave her all day in the cellar without
getting her to say 'Yes', she would sooner sleep there."

Such a temperament would need firm and wise
guidance to protect it from the obvious pitfalls. Her sister
Marie gave little Thérèse and Céline a chaplet of beads
upon which to count their sacrifices. Every time they
made a little sacrifice of their wills they were to move a
bead across. The two little sisters encouraged each other
in this practice. "Thus", she tells us, "I acquired the habit
of refraining from complaint when anything belonging to

me was taken away: also when accused unjustly, I preferred to remain silent rather than to defend myself". So in the earliest years she learnt the self-sacrifice and self-control in little things so essential to all holiness.

Thérèse delighted in her home, revelled in her toys and games, but supremely she loved nature. On the outskirts of the town her father owned a small house surrounded by a large garden. Here it was little Thérèse's delight to play, and from this garden she would return laden with flowers. From the first her bouquets were always of the simple wild flowers, daisies, buttercups, and wild poppies, just as she had gathered them here and there along her path. "I remember the Sunday walks when our dear mother always came with us. I can still feel the impression made on my childish heart at the sight of the fields bright with cornflowers, poppies, and marguerites. Even at that age I loved far-stretching views, sunlit spaces, and stately trees: in a word all nature charmed me and lifted up my soul to Heaven". She seems even at this early age to have understood the symbolism of flowers offered in token of love, for these flowers were invariably laid at the statue of Our Lady, a first token of that complete oblation of her soul and life which was to come.

Thus passed the first years of her life. But now God Himself was to take the formation of this little soul into His own hands by means of suffering, by which alone can Saints be made.

When little Thérèse was only four and a half years old her mother was stricken with a fatal illness and, after months of great suffering, passed to her reward on 28th August 1877. The little family was left desolate. Before the mortal remains of her mother disappeared from the eyes of the little one her father took her in his arms. "Come" he said, "kiss your mother for the last time". She did so without uttering a word or shedding a tear. After the mother's funeral the family had returned home plunged in sorrow. The whole five of them stood together in a group, mutely gazing at one another in their grief. The maid seeing them said: "Poor little children, you have no mother". Whereupon little Thérèse, flinging herself in Pauline's arms, said: "Pauline will be my mother".

The effect of this great sorrow on little Thérèse was tremendous. To her sensitive nature the shock was overwhelming. Her disposition completely changed, instead of being lively and demonstrative she became timid, shy, reserved, and extremely sensitive, and she would very easily burst into tears; it was not till ten years later when she was fourteen years old that she fully regained her old gaiety.

School Days

Soon after their mother's death, M. Martin moved from Alençon to Lisieux in order that his children might be under the influence of his sister-in-law, Madame Guérin. In their new home, Les Buissonnets, a charming little house set in a quiet garden, the home life with its Catholic piety and its human affection was resumed. But one thing was for ever altered for Thérèse, her mother was in heaven and heaven was her real home. Her home on earth was but a passing, broken thing. The mother she loved so dearly was in heaven. So the transient joys of this world – though she had the greatest appreciation of them, for Thérèse was no ready-made ascetic – gradually became of little account compared to those things unseen which are eternal. It is important to realise this, for it explains the rapid growth of the soul and the unusual sense of detachment from the world which was so soon to develop.

To Pauline fell the task of mothering her little sister. As a teacher she was firm as she was devoted. She required a definite amount of study to be done, and if application to work was remiss the evening walk was invariably cancelled. Pauline never went back on a decision once given, and M. Martin, at whatever cost, ratified her verdict. It was during one of these evening walks that her father took Thérèse to pay a visit to the Blessed Sacrament in the Carmel chapel. "Look, little one", he said, pointing to the grille, "behind there are the holy nuns who are always praying". It was in that chapel nine years later that the little one was to take the veil. During these walks the sight of the venerable father holding by the hand his little daughter often attracted the notice of passers-by. Thérèse, with her long golden hair, her sweet smile, and clear deep eyes, was growing into a beautiful girl. One day a lady accompanied by her husband could not refrain from saying in a low tone as they passed, "What a pretty little girl!" and she asked M. Martin if she belonged to him. The father, though pleased, signed to them not to address compliments to his little daughter. Sometimes her father took her with him fishing. She would sit in the fields amid the flowers. In her own words: "I listened to distant far-off sounds and the murmuring of the wind. Earth seemed a place of exile and I dreamed of Heaven". From these walks she would return laden with wild flowers with which she used to deck Our Lady's statue.

The graces resulting from union with God were vividly increasing in this simple child of just five years old who sought our Divine Saviour with all her soul. In little Thérèse's quest for God during these days at Les Buissonnets, it was the dearly loved mother, who had been so swiftly torn from her, who was still her teacher. "As I grew up", she declares, "I loved God more and more, and I frequently made Him the offering of my heart, using the words my mother had taught me. I strove to please Jesus in all my actions and I guarded with great care against ever offending Him".

Thus the first three years of Thérèse's life after her mother's death were spent in the loving atmosphere of Les Buissonnets. But the time had come – Thérèse was now eight years old – for her to go to school. The school chosen was that of the

Benedictine Abbey of Notre Dame du Pré, situated in a suburb of Lisieux some considerable distance from Les Buissonnets. On account of her remarkable ability she was placed in a class composed of girls much older than herself, some of them indeed fourteen years of age, and even so she soon succeeded in finding herself among the first. Human nature is the same the whole world over, and it was impossible for this to take place without causing jealousy among the other girls. Added to this, the spiritual character of little Thérèse made her an object of interest to the nuns: this only made matters worse. Again the very nature of Thérèse made it difficult for her to enter the world of strenuous games in which it was so easy for her schoolfellows to excel, but in which she was never able to take any serious interest. Clever at her work, highly thought of by the nuns, not good at games – all this was to create a situation very difficult for Thérèse. How did she meet it? With all her excessive sensitiveness she suffered acutely, unable to defend herself she became reticent, and more and more found her refuge in thinking of that very world which made this one so difficult for her. She tells us herself: "One of the other children seeing me so young and almost always first at composition and loved by all the nuns became jealous and made me pay in many ways for my little successes. In my timidity, self-defence was impossible and I simply cried in silence".

Had Thérèse been a person with a smaller capacity for affection it would not have been so difficult, but it was just the fact that her heart was so capable of loving that made this loneliness and misunderstanding to which she was subjected so hard to bear. Her affectionate nature was cut to the heart. Years after she tells us herself: "I chose as friends two little girls of my own age... One of them had to stay at home for some months; while she was away I thought about her very often and on her return I showed how pleased I was. However all I got was a glance of indifference, my friendship was not appreciated. I felt this very keenly and I no longer sought an affection which had proved so inconstant. Nevertheless I still love my little school friend and continue to pray for her. For God has given me a faithful heart, and when once I love, I love for ever". These last words are true self-revelation. If Thérèse was detached from the outer world, she was never detached from human love. When, in later life, she cut herself off from intercourse with those she loved in the world, it was not love she renounced but the delights of love. Her love was genuine and therefore unswervingly loyal. This was equally true of her love for other people and of her love for her Lord. "My little way is all love", she said. It was – all love, love to Him, which never wavered in any stress of body, mind or spirit.

So these incidents of her early childhood, trivial as many of them are in themselves, are illuminating as we watch a Saint in the making. Through all these events, big and small, fortunate and unfortunate; even through the misunderstanding and thoughtlessness of those surrounding her, often of those to whom she was really dear; even through her own reactions – unfortunate as they might appear to some; through all this God was fashioning His Saint.

Thérèse had hardly been at school a year when Pauline, her beloved "little mother", entered Carmel. We have seen the effect of the loss of her first mother on Thérèse. The suffering caused now by the loss of her second "little mother" was more than she could stand. Pauline then was going away for ever. The family reunions at Les Buissonnets would be no more. Though Thérèse never mentioned her school troubles at home it was these family reunions in the evening which made it easier for her to bear them. Now these were to be shattered. The first visits to the Carmel only increased her suffering, for she could only see her "little mother" for two or three minutes at the most, and that behind a grille instead of resting on her knee. "I who had been accustomed to talk with my little mother of all that was in my heart could now scarcely snatch two or three minutes at the end of the family visits, even those short minutes were passed in tears, I went away with my heart torn with grief. I kept saying from the depth of my heart 'Pauline is lost to me!'"

Her health, which had long been precarious, was not proof against this trial. She was seized every evening with violent trembling. Terrifying visions drew from her cries of distress which struck fear as much as sorrow into those who heard them. She would try to throw herself out of bed, and her face, usually so sweet and serene, wore an indescribable expression of terror. The doctor declared: "Science is powerless before this phenomenon, there is nothing that can be done". It seemed as if the Evil One was allowed to take possession of her. Despairing of earthly remedies, M. Martin requested a novena of Masses for the cure of his little daughter at the church of Notre Dame des Victories in Paris. On the Sunday evening during the novena Thérèse was taken much worse, and her three sisters, convinced that she would die, fell on their knees before the statue of Our Lady which stood beside her bed. With them, the sick child turned her eyes upon the statue. Let her tell the rest in her own words: "All at once the statue became animated. Our Lady became so beautiful that I shall never find words to express that heavenly loveliness. Her countenance breathed sweetness, goodness, and unspeakable tenderness, but what penetrated to the depths of my soul was her ravishing smile. Then all my pain vanished: two great tears fell silently from my eyes. They were tears of unalloyed heavenly joy. The Blessed Virgin came towards me. She smiled on me. 'How happy I am' I thought, 'but I will tell no one, for then my happiness would vanish'. Then I lowered my eyes and without any effort recognised my dear sisters". Thérèse was completely cured.

This cure was not only confined to her body, for during this illness she had developed spiritually as well, and, young as she was, she had begun to learn the lesson of detachment from the natural affection which had cost her so dear. Henceforth her visits to her little mother at Carmel were ones of pure joy. "What happy moments they were for us both, we had so much to say, we had both suffered so much; my heart was so full that I could hardly speak". This seems to have been clearly the result of her illness.

Before her return to school, M. Martin, in order to completely restore her health, took little Thérèse for a holiday in the country. He took her to some friends near Alençon, who received them in their respective châteaux of St Denis and Grogny. The season was favourable and the scenery lovely: in this beautiful setting Thérèse was petted, made much of, and admired. She admits that she felt the charm of the world and its attractions. "At ten years of age the heart is easily fascinated and I confess that in my case this kind of life had its charms. And yet death has come to many people I knew then, young, rich, and happy. I recall to mind the delightful places where they lived and ask myself where they are now and what profit they derive today from the beautiful houses and grounds where I saw them living. Perhaps Our Lord wished me to know something of the world ... so that I might choose more deliberately the way in which I was to follow Him".

First Communion

From the very first Thérèse had shown a great love for the Blessed Sacrament and a great longing for her first Communion. When quite a tiny child she slipped out of the front door and started off in pouring rain after having been told it was too wet for her to go to Mass. She begged Marie and Pauline to let her creep up between them to the altar rails at the Midnight Mass. "Nobody will see me", she said. One day when out for a walk in Lisieux she saw the Bishop on the other side of the street and entreated her sisters to let her go and ask his permission to hasten the day of her first Communion. Now the long desired day was drawing near. Thérèse was eleven years old. In the retreat by which she prepared her soul for the great event she made two resolutions. (i) I will never give way to discouragement. (ii) I will endeavour to humble my pride. These two resolutions give us a little glimpse into her character, showing that intense sensitiveness which might so easily have given way to discouragement and, on the other hand, that force and strength which might so easily have become pride. They show too what is most remarkable in a child of eleven, her self-knowledge. At last the happy day dawned. Let her describe it in her own words: "How sweet was the first embrace of Jesus! It was indeed an embrace of love. I felt that I was loved, and I said 'I love Thee and I give myself to Thee for ever'. Jesus asked nothing of me and claimed no sacrifice. For a long time He and little Thérèse had known and understood one another. My joy became so intense it could not be restrained and my tears overflowed. My companions were astonished and asked each other, 'Why did she cry? Because neither her mother nor her dearly loved Carmelite sister were here?' And none understood that all the joy of Heaven had come down into one heart, and that this heart, exiled, weak, and mortal as it was, could not contain it without tears". The happy day ended with a visit to her dear Pauline. M. Martin took his daughter in the evening to see her little mother who that very day had been professed in the Carmel Convent. This time there were no tears of separation, but rather a quiet determination on the part of the little one to join Pauline as soon as she could. So closed that memorable day, 8th May 1884, a date destined to be famous throughout the Catholic world.

Two years later M. Martin took his little daughter away from the convent school in order that she might have private lessons with a lady of good position in the town and that at the same time she might come into closer contact with the world. Here we find Thérèse seated before a desk in an antiquely furnished room where numbers of well-meaning ladies came daily in search of distraction. Some would remark on the new pupil's beautiful hair, others would ask in a whisper who was this pretty little girl. Thérèse, though apparently studying, heard and understood all. "Such remarks, the more flattering because I was not meant to hear them, gave me a feeling of pleasure ... if my heart had not been lifted up towards God from the first moment of consciousness, if the world had smiled on me from the beginning of my life, what should I have become?" Thérèse was now nearly fourteen, and Marie, who had been her confidante during the last years, judged her now able to bear another separation and entered the Carmel, October 1886.

It now remained to overcome finally that extreme sensitiveness which had handicapped Thérèse ever since her mother died. It needed a little miracle, for nothing seemed able to help her. On Christmas Day, 1886, Thérèse, on her return from the Midnight Mass, found her shoes in the chimney corner filled with presents, a custom usual among French children. Her father generally liked to watch her enjoyment as she took out each present from her shoes. On this occasion he seemed vexed and said: "Really Thérèse is too old for all this". Thérèse heard him say this. Céline, knowing how sensitive she was and fearing she might cry, urged her to wait. But Thérèse went straight to her shoes and took out each present one by one without the smallest tremor. Through this incident, apparently so trivial, Thérèse had regained once and for all the strength of mind which she had lost at the age of four and a half. "On this night of grace in one instant Our Lord, satisfied with my goodwill, accomplished the work which I had not been able to do during all these years". This complete mastery of herself, given her in such a clearly supernatural manner, and which she was never again to lose even in moments of greatest trial and suffering, St Thérèse always regarded as one of Our Lord's greatest gifts to her: she goes so far as to describe it as her "Conversion".

Apostolic Zeal

Fourteen years of age and completely restored to health and gaiety, the thoughts of little Thérèse were turning ever more definitely towards Carmel. What was the reason? Was it to hide herself away from the problems and temptations of life in order to live a life of selfish isolation? Far from it. Her motive was that in Carmel she might give herself more completely to Our Lord for the salvation of souls. One Sunday as she closed her book at Mass a picture of Our Saviour on the Cross slipped out from the pages, showing one of the divine hands pierced and bleeding. "I experienced then", she tells us, "a new and expressible feeling ... I resolved that in spirit I would stand continually at the foot of the Cross to receive the divine dew of salvation and to pour it out upon souls ... I felt myself devoured with the thirst for souls".

In the latter part of June, 1887, everybody was speaking of the horrible murder of two women and a girl in the rue Montaigne, Paris, by a man named Pranzini. The assassin showed no sign of repentance and refused all help from religion. Little Thérèse was seized with unbounded compassion. She started to pray for him with all her soul, and begged of God a sign to show that her prayers were answered. "This is my first sinner, for that reason I ask a sign of repentance for my own consolation". Each day she eagerly looked at the paper for news of her protégé. On September 1st she saw the account of his death. Struggling with his executioners and repelling the priest, he was laid on the guillotine; when all of a sudden, just before the fatal stroke, he asked for the chaplain's crucifix and kissed it three times. On reading this, little Thérèse had to run out of the room to hide her emotion. She had been given her sign! In her own words: "The lips of my 'first child' were pressed to the divine wounds: what a sweet response. My desire to save souls increased each day after this wonderful grace". When later in the year she went on the pilgrimage to Rome a fellow pilgrim lent her the annals of some missionary nuns. She accepted them with enthusiasm, and then gave them to her sister, saying: "I will not read them, for I have too ardent a desire to consecrate myself to works of zeal, but I wish to be hidden in a cloister so as to give myself more completely to God". She confided to Céline that the reason for this preference was "in order to suffer more, and by this means to gain more souls to Jesus", and especially to pray for priests and to sacrifice herself for the interests of Holy Church.

Forcing the Gates of Carmel

How was she to achieve the overwhelming desire of her soul? The Mother Prioress and her eldest sister, Marie, thought she was still too young. "I found but one person", she declares, "to encourage me in my vocation: my dear Pauline." Thérèse must now take the issue into her own hands. The prospects were enough to daunt any heart, let alone that of a child of fourteen and a half. Her courage was amazing. The first great difficulty was that of leaving her father. He was then sixty-four years of age and none too strong, having had a slight stroke. The thought of leaving him in loneliness made her tremble. She chose the day of Pentecost to make her great disclosure, and prayed to the Holy Spirit for fortitude.

It was a beautiful summer evening and M. Martin was seated in the garden. Quietly, and with her eyes filled with tears, she sat down silently beside him. "What is it, my little Queen, tell me", he said, drawing her close to him: and, rising to hide his emotion, he commenced to walk slowly up the garden path, keeping his arm close around her. Amid tears Thérèse revealed her secret – she felt drawn to Carmel and she desired to enter soon within its walls. For a moment he was overcome, then he listened to her reasons, which she, now more sure of herself, laid before him with calmness. Then approaching a wall where grew some tiny white flowers which in form and shape resembled a lily, he plucked one and offered it to his daughter as a symbol of the virginal purity that she wished to consecrate to God. "I received this little flower as a relic and noticed that in gathering it my father had pulled it up by the roots without breaking them: it seemed destined to live on, but in other more fertile soil. Papa had just done the same for me. He allowed me to leave the sweet valley where I had passed the first years of my life for the mountain of Carmel". Had he but known it, her father in giving her that little flower was giving his daughter the name by which she would be known and loved throughout the world.

These two hearts were henceforth united in the aspiration towards the same ideal: the step which had cost Thérèse the most had been successfully taken.

The second obstacle to be overcome was the opposition of the ecclesiastical superiors. The Mother Prioress, who at first had been doubtful as to the wisdom of admitting Thérèse so young, was now quite disposed to welcome her. But before doing so she must consult the ecclesiastical Superior, Canon Delatroitte, the Bishop's representative.

Holding very strongly, as he did, that nobody should be allowed to enter Carmel till her twenty-first year, his refusal to the Mother Prioress was absolute and final. There was nothing for it but that M. Martin should accompany his little daughter for a personal interview with the redoubtable Canon. A short and decisive "No" to the opening words of Thérèse cut short the little speech she had prepared. But in parting with her the conscientious priest remarked: "However I am only the delegate of the Bishop. If he allows you to enter I shall have no more to say". This gave Thérèse a ray of hope. She would appeal to the Bishop. Once more her father accompanied her. The interview was arranged for them by the Vicar-General, the Abbé Révérony. It was a great ordeal for little Thérèse. So that she might not appear quite so young, she put her hair up for the first time. Till this hour she had never gone to visit anyone without her sisters, and now she was to begin by visiting a bishop. Added to this, she who never spoke except to reply to the questions of others found herself obliged to explain before a prelate her reason for seeking a strange and almost unheard-of favour.

It was an immense trial of her courage. The Abbé Révérony, who met them, noticing the tears in her eyes, said to her: "Ah, I see diamonds! You must not show these to the Bishop". There were three large armchairs in front of a brightly burning fire. Thérèse was told to sit in the central chair. In her own words: "I found myself buried in a monumental chair where four little girls like me could have sat at their ease, more at their ease than I, for I was far from feeling at home". She made her appeal and gave her reasons. The Bishop listened kindly and, after talking for a while with her, said he must delay his answer and in the meantime must consult the dreaded Superior, Canon

Delatroitte. Nothing could have been worse. "Disregarding M. Révérony's warning", says Thérèse, "I did more than show my diamonds to the Bishop, I gave them – shedding tears." The Bishop was moved, and spoke tenderly to her. He then took her round the garden. The audience was finished. Thérèse had accomplished nothing.

One last resource remained, a personal appeal to the Holy Father, Pope Leo XIII. This was made possible by the fact that M. Martin had already arranged to take Céline and Thérèse on a pilgrimage to the Holy City. This, apart from her special intention, was to be a great experience for Thérèse.

The train passed through Switzerland. The heart of Thérèse was captivated by the scenery. The mountains with their precipices, the chalets and the graceful belfries, the immense lakes shining in the setting sun, entranced her. Let us hear her own words: "I said to myself: 'Later on, in the hour of trial, when, a prisoner in the Carmel, I shall be able to see only a little corner of the heavens, I will recall this scene and the remembrance will give me courage. I shall no longer be preoccupied about my own petty interests when thinking on the greatness and power of God. I will love Him alone and shall not be so unfortunate as to become attached to trifles now that my heart foresees something of what He has in store for those who love Him".

Nothing reveals the failings of good people more than the close intimacy of life on a pilgrimage. Among the pilgrims were many priests. Edifying though they were, they were not wholly freed from every weakness of human nature. "During that month", she says, "I met many holy priests, and I have seen that if their sublime dignity has raised them above the Angels, they are as men still subject to human weakness and frailty. If these holy priests, whom Jesus in the Gospel calls the salt of the earth, show that they have need of prayer, what of those who are lukewarm?" It was thus she realised that prayer for priests was one of the highest services rendered by Carmel.

But the journey and the pilgrimage were to bring her into touch with a variety of laymen as well as with a variety of priests. This she had realised before leaving, and she had offered special prayers for protection and guidance to Our Lady and her shrine in Our Lady of Victories, Paris, and to St Joseph, the father and protector of virgins. When the pilgrims alighted from the train at Bologna, they found themselves surrounded by a crowd of boisterous students. One of them, attracted by Thérèse's good looks, seized hold of her and, in a moment, lifted her across the railway line. Quickly freeing herself from his hold, she turned on him a look which made him shrink away in confusion. Later in the pilgrimage a more subtle difficulty came her way. One of the pilgrims, a young man of good family, showed her rather too marked attentions. She met his advances with complete reserve, not because she was by nature austere or on this particular occasion unresponsive to the charm of the individual with whom she was dealing, but because she was already so entirely convinced of God's Will for her, and because, as always, she was unswervingly faithful in following it. "Oh, it is indeed time that Jesus took me away from the world ... I feel that my heart would easily let itself be taken captive by affection".

These incidents of the journey and pilgrimage, like those of her childhood, are revealing. Here is a soul at once very human and truly consecrated. She shows neither contempt for her young fellow pilgrim nor self-satisfaction because she has attracted him, but simply a quiet determination in no way to deviate from that path which she believes it to be God's Will she should tread. She feels no scorn of the good priests for their failings – only a realisation of their need for intercession, and of the yet greater need of more unworthy priests. The stupendous glory of the Alps fills her whole being with delight, but it does more; she reaches out through and beyond it to the thought of that beauty which eye has not seen nor ear heard nor man's heart conceived. And so she faces calmly the prospect of being shut away from much of the beauty of this world for the sake of that "Beauty which doth leave all beauty plain". In all this we see this child of God relating every experience to her Heavenly Father, just as any little child turns instinctively in everything to his mother – that is, we see her already following faithfully that Little Way of Spiritual Childhood which it is her Mission to teach us all.

In Rome

In Rome itself the monument which stirred the heart of Thérèse most was the Coliseum, that great amphitheatre where the early martyrs had so profusely shed their blood: it was the scene of a daring escapade on the part of the two sisters. Ignoring the warnings of the guide and the cries of their father, Thérèse and Céline slipped through the barricade and, climbing amid the excavations and amid ruins which crumbled beneath their feet, scrambled perilously to a point many feet below, to the spot where so many martyrs had won their crown. Thérèse describes how deeply moved she was when their lips touched the spot sanctified by the blood of martyrs. Then she says: "I asked the grace that I too might be a martyr for Jesus and I felt deep down in my heart that my prayer was heard". Collecting a few stones as relics, they made their way back to their party who, admiring their courage, had not the heart to scold them.

But the supreme object of the pilgrimage was the audience with the Holy Father at which Thérèse hoped to make her supreme appeal. November 20th was the day chosen for the audience. Exactly at eight Leo XIII appeared. Having offered the Holy Sacrifice, he went to his seat in the audience chamber to receive the pilgrims. Each member of the pilgrimage was presented in turn. In the presence of the high dignitaries surrounding the Holy Father, in the presence of many Monsignori and other prelates,

surrounded by the Noble Guard and in the sight and hearing
of over a hundred pilgrims, would the little child of fourteen
dare to ask of Leo XIII the request which had been deferred
by the Bishop of Bayeaux? To do so would demand nothing
less than real heroism.

When M. Révérony, who was introducing the pilgrims,
saw the two sisters approach the Pontifical Throne, he
announced in a loud voice that nobody was to speak to the
Holy Father. Thérèse looked imploringly for a sign from
Céline. "Speak", said her elder sister. A moment after
Thérèse is at the feet of Leo XIII. She quickly kisses the
Pontiff's foot, grasps his extended hand: then with eyes
filled with tears exclaims: "Most Holy Father, I have a great
favour to ask". The Pope bent down his head till it touched
Thérèse's veil. His dark piercing eyes sought to read those
of the child. She continued: "Most Holy Father, in honour
of your Jubilee, permit me to enter Carmel at fifteen". Here
M. Révérony intervened. "Most Holy Father", he said, "this
is a child who desires the life of Carmel, but the Superiors
are at the moment considering the question". "Very well,
my child", said His Holiness, "do whatever the Superiors
shall decide". Clasping her hands and resting them on his
knee little Thérèse makes her last despairing appeal: "O
Holy Father, if only you say 'Yes' everyone else will
agree". Leo XIII, looking at her fixedly and with kindness,
said in an earnest voice: "Well, well, my child, you will
enter if it be God's Will". The other pilgrims were waiting

their turn. Thérèse was about to speak again when two of the Noble Guard told her to rise. As she still remained kneeling they took her by the arms, and M. Révérony had to come to their aid before she would leave her place at the Sovereign Pontiff's feet. Just as she was forced to rise, the Holy Father gently placed his hand on her lips, then lifted it to bless her, following her with his eyes for quite a long time. It was over: the long weary journey had apparently failed in its object. The poor child retired in desolation and overwhelmed in tears. She had done all in her power to answer Heaven's call. The Almighty had judged fit to overthrow her calculations and hopes: the trial was a very hard one, and yet in her innermost soul she was at peace, for she had done what she could.

On her return to Lisieux she hastened to the convent to tell her sisters the result of the journey. Her sister Pauline, now Sister Agnes, who had always encouraged her desire for Carmel, advised her to write to the Bishop, as he had promised her a written reply. This she did, but he remained silent.

On 1st January 1888, however, Thérèse received a letter from the Prioress saying that the Bishop had sanctioned her entry to the convent, but that it was thought better to defer her entrance till after Lent. At last the gates of Carmel were open to her, and the few months that still remained before she could enter were used by her as months of special preparation.

April the 9th was the date chosen for her entrance. On the evening of April the 8th the family, consisting of the father and the three sisters, with Thérèse's uncle and aunt and their two girls, gathered together for the last time in the home which she loved so dearly. Everything in it was precious to her: the garden where she had so often played, the hearth round which they had spent so many winter evenings, these indeed must have called to her heart; but how much more must she have felt the separation from the family whom she had loved so dearly and must now leave behind. In her own words: "Just when one would wish to be forgotten, words of the deepest tenderness were on all lips as though to make the sacrifice of separation more keenly felt than ever". The following morning the family assisted at High Mass. When Mass was over Thérèse walked towards the cloister door. Those around her were crying; she herself shed no tears. But, as she tells us: "My heart beat so violently that I asked myself whether I was not about to die". She knelt to receive her father's blessing, then, rising, she entered the open door – the goal of all her struggles, the object of all her sacrifices and sufferings, the supreme desire of her heroic heart. "At last", she tells us, "the doors of Carmel closed behind me, and there I received the embraces of the two beloved sisters who had each been a mother to me, and of a new family whose loving devotedness is unknown to the world".

In Carmel

Novitiate and Profession

"Now I am here for ever". These were St Thérèse's words as for the first time she entered her little cell, which charmed her above all because of its cold, bare walls and its rugged simplicity. Everything spoke to her of that detachment and that sacrifice which she longed for as being the supreme means of union with her Lord, so that she might become His instrument for saving souls.

How was this to happen? We might have thought that her life in Carmel, with her two sisters, would have many natural attractions which would make that life easy for her. But this was not so. From the very beginning the only attractions that God gave her or that she allowed herself were supernatural, attained nearly always at the cost of the natural.

While the doors of Carmel were still open, and her father and her family standing by, the old ecclesiastical Superior, still doubting the wisdom of such an early entry, said in a loud voice to the Mother Prioress: "I trust she may not disappoint your hopes, but I remind you that, if it should turn out otherwise, the responsibility will be yours alone". This was the first mortification she received in the cloister to which she had come to pray, to suffer, and make reparation. From the outset the new postulant met with misunderstanding. The Mother Prioress, Mother Mary Gonzaga, treated her severely – partly on principle because, as she said, "Dispensations are not for a soul of such metal", which shows that very early she noted the spiritual capacity of her new child: and also because she was by temperament unable to understand Thérèse's particularly sensitive nature. The other superior under whose direct care the Saint found herself was the novice mistress. Here again was an occasion of great suffering. Mother Mary of the Angels, as she was named, was an exemplary religious; but, with all the goodwill in the world, she too was unable to understand the new postulant. It was just one of those cases in which it was utterly impossible for one soul to speak to another. In the words of St Thérèse: "Though I loved her I could not explain myself to her; words failed me". So the time of spiritual direction became a veritable martyrdom. For both these good religious Thérèse, from the first, had felt a great attraction; years afterwards, in writing her autobiography, she says how clearly providential this suffering was, for otherwise she could so easily have rested in natural affections; thus her heart, having been saved from stopping short at human affection in the world, might easily have become captive to some natural friendship in the cloister.

We might have expected that she would have found some consolation and help from her confessor. The chaplain of the

Carmel at the time of her entry suffered from ill-health, and it was impossible to get from him the direction which she needed. Besides him, she saw only the preacher of the retreat. One of these, Father Blino, of the Society of Jesus, completely misunderstood her ardour. Her outbursts of love were regarded by him as pride and presumption. "Confine yourself", he said, "to the correction of your faults and subdue your rash desires". There was however one Father who saw what others had failed to see, that here was a soul destined to be a saint. This was Père Pichon. On leaving, the Father said to her: "My child, may Our Saviour be always your Superior and your Novice Master". No sooner had this good Father taken charge of her soul than he was sent off to Canada, and once again Thérèse was left alone.

In this situation we might have expected her heart to turn to her sisters who in the years gone by had guided her so faithfully along her spiritual pilgrimage. But, knowing as she did, that perfect charity required the sacrifice of natural affection, at any rate in its external manifestations, Thérèse, loving and sensitive as she was, never sought the company of her two sisters, Agnes and Marie. At recreation she took her place beside whoever came first, or next to anyone who might seem to her forlorn.

She seems to have drawn her spiritual guidance and her supernatural consolations above all from three sources. First the Divine Office; that is to say, the prayers and psalms and readings of Scripture which form the greater part of the prayer of a Carmelite, offered together with the rest of the Community in their chapel. Of this she says: "I can say truly that the Divine Office has been at the same time my joy and my martyrdom. For I had a great desire to recite it without fault, yet in spite of all my application I made mistakes". The second source of her inspiration she found in Saint Thérèse and St John of the Cross, the classics of the Carmelite Order. She loved the beautiful and mystical lyrics of the latter saint and was deeply imbued with his teaching. Even more than here she found a mine of treasure in the Imitation, which she knew by heart from childhood and which was her constant companion. But the supreme source of all were the Gospels. Soon after her entrance to the convent she found a little volume of the Four Gospels small enough for her to carry next her heart. Later on, during the time when she was undergoing severe temptations against Faith, it was in this little book that she wrote the entire Credo in her blood; and, in defiance of the Evil One, she died with it next her heart. Writing to her Mother Prioress she said: "It is the Gospels which above all occupy my mind during mental prayer. From them I draw everything necessary for my poor little soul. In them I ever discover new lights, hidden and mysterious meanings".

The first great event after her entrance was her Clothing, which took place on January 10th, 1889. This was delayed three months, apparently at the instigation of the still sceptical ecclesiastical Superior. This delay was just another of those trials which met her all along her path. Her Clothing was preceded by a retreat. Here at least we should have expected some consolation. But all was darkness and aridity. "In my soul's intercourse with Jesus", she tells us, "there is nothing but dryness and sleep". This does not cause her to despair. On the contrary she offers it all to Him as the best possible token of her love. "Everything shall be for Him, everything; and even when I have nothing to give Him, as this evening, I will offer Him that nothing".

Before her entry into Carmel her father had suffered his first attack of paralysis. He was however able to be with her at her Clothing. He was waiting for her at the enclosure door, where, pressing her to his heart, he then took her by the arm, and they made their solemn entrance into the chapel. This was the day of his triumph, his last feast on earth. All his offerings were made. His children belonged to God; for Céline had just told him that she too desired to enter Carmel.

Snow had always had a particular attraction for Thérèse. She was born amid the snow of winter. She had a great desire to see the earth clad in white on the day of her Clothing. But the extreme mildness of the day made it seem impossible. On re-entering the cloister after the ceremony she found it covered with snow. Ever after, this was referred to as the little miracle.

But now fell the blow which was to flood Thérèse and her family in long, lasting, and overwhelming sorrow. Their father had a second attack of paralysis, so bad that he had to be taken to a nursing home where he remained for three years. The paralysis affected his brain, and he who had so tenderly watched over his daughters was now at times unable even to recognise them. The blow fell heavily on Thérèse who had always loved him with a very special love. She simply says: "Words could not express my agony. I shall not try to describe it". Yet once again the soul of the young Carmelite rose triumphant through it all, finding in it the special mark of her Saviour's love, calling her and her sisters through this suffering to a freedom from all earthly affections so that they might love Him for Himself alone. "The three years", she writes, "of my father's martyrdom seem to me the dearest and most fruitful of my life. I would not exchange them for divine ecstasies". Again, to Céline, she says: "Far from making any complaint to Our Saviour for the grace He has sent us, I cannot comprehend the infinite Love that has urged Him to deal thus with us. Our father must be greatly loved by God, since he has so much to suffer. What a delight to share in his humiliation".

When the year's novitiate was over, and the time had come for her to take the final vows, the still implacable ecclesiastical Superior opposed it, and for nine months it was delayed.

But at last the day arrived, and on 8th September 1890, Thérèse made her solemn Profession. Once more it was a time of darkness. But this absence of consolation was but in accordance with the way in which her Divine Master had led her from the moment of her entry, and only made the gift of herself more perfect. Never did she love Him more wholeheartedly than in this path of darkness which He had chosen for her. She tells us how, in her retreat, her Saviour led her by the hand along a subterranean way "where it is neither hot nor cold, where the sun never shines, into which no wind nor rain find entrance", where the Face of her Lord appeared merely as a half-veiled light. Of this retreat she writes to her sister: "I am grateful to Jesus for making me walk in darkness. I am in profound peace. Willingly I consent to remain during the whole of my religious life in this sombre tunnel into which He has made me enter. I desire only that my darkness may obtain light for sinners. I am happy, yes, truly happy, in having no consolations. I should feel ashamed if my love resembled that of earthly fiancées who look for presents from the hand of their betrothed, or eagerly watch his face for the loving smile that delights them ... Jesus! I would so love Him, love Him as He has never yet been loved".

The night before her Profession she was attacked by an overwhelming temptation. The devil endeavoured to persuade her that she was not called to the religious life and should return to the world. So strong was her temptation that she was driven to tell her novice mistress, who reassured her, and thus she regained her peace. "On the morning of 8th September", she says, "rivers of peace inundated my soul, and in that Peace which passeth all understanding I made my Holy Vows. At the end of that happy day it was without sadness that I laid my crown of roses, according to custom, at the feet of the Blessed Virgin. I felt that time would never take from me my joy".

On 24th September Thérèse completed the great Act of Profession, according to the Carmelite custom, by taking the veil.

Such was the soul that Our Lord chose to take to Himself to be His spouse on that September morning. Gradually He had drawn her from every created thing and from every human affection – not that she should love her dear ones less, but that, loving Him above all, she should love them more than ever before. This way of darkness, of mysterious and hidden suffering, was exactly the way in which a soul capable of such love and such sacrifice can alone be developed. The simple directness of her love inspired her to rise through all trials of her life in Carmel to a degree of union with her Lord which a less simple soul could never have achieved. Was it not also the very foundation of her mission as a Carmelite to save souls? "In the solemn examination before my Profession I declared, as was customary, the reason for my entry into the Carmel: 'I have come to save souls, especially to pray for priests'. One cannot attain the end without adopting the means. And as Our Blessed Lord made me understand that it was by this grace He would give me souls, the stronger grew my attraction to suffering. For five years this way was mine, but I alone knew it. It was precisely the flower I wished to offer Jesus, the hidden flower which keeps its perfume only for Heaven".

The Saint's Spirituality

Thus far we have followed St Thérèse up to her Profession, and we have seen how Our Lord trained her in the school of loneliness and sacrifice. We have seen how in her Profession she offered herself with such generosity to the love of her Heavenly Spouse. How then is that offering to be made perfect? How will her soul be developed along the road to perfection by Our Lord, by His grace? That is to be our study now.[1] She must tell us in her own words. There are two passages where she describes her "little way", as she calls it, of spirituality. "When I read certain treatises where many obstacles to perfection are shown, my poor mind grows tired very quickly. I close the learned book that wearies my head and dries up my heart, and I take instead the Holy Scripture.

---

[1] The Little Way may be studied at greater length in *The Message of St Thérèse of Lisieux* (by the same writer), which should be read in conjunction with this pamphlet (CTS booklet D 331).

Then everything appears to me in a clear light. A single word opens out infinite horizons to my soul. Perfection seems easy to reach. I realise that it is sufficient to recognise one's nothingness and to abandon oneself as a child in the Arms of God". The second passage is even more detailed. Writing to her Mother Prioress she says: "You know I have always longed to be a saint, but I found it impossible. We live in a century of inventions. The trouble of walking upstairs exists no longer; in the houses of the rich, the lift replaces the stairs. I too should like to find a lift to raise me to Jesus, for I am too little to ascend the steep steps of perfection. Then I sought in the Scriptures some indication of this lift, the object of my desires; and I read these words from the mouth of Eternal Wisdom: 'Whosoever is a little one, let him come to me'. 'As one whom the mother caresseth, so will I comfort you'. 'You shall be carried at the breasts, and upon the knees shall they caress you'. Never have more tender or melodious words gladdened my soul. Thine Arms, O Jesus, shall be the lift that shall raise me to Heaven. For this I have no need of becoming greater. On the contrary I must be little and become even smaller".

These passages combined with Our Lord's words: "Unless you are converted and become as little children you cannot enter the Kingdom of Heaven" are the sources from which she learned the little way which God had designed for the perfection of her soul. It was the Gospel itself, which preaches unceasingly the way of abandonment and childlike love towards our Heavenly Father, that she found her inspiration.

We will now watch as she walks along this way of childlike abandonment.

This loving abandonment transfigured the whole of her life. She moved along her little way, a humble and confident child of her Heavenly Father, and this loving abandonment showed itself in every single aspect of her life. And, as little children can only express their love by little things, so it was with her. Every little detail of her life became an expression of her love. Because she was so little nothing was too small. And this gives the clue to the first great secret, namely, the preciousness of little things as expressions of our love to the Heavenly Father. Every detail of her daily routine, whether it was in the laundry or the sacristy, in the garden or in the chapel, whether it was sweeping the passages, cleaning the refectory or working in the kitchen, all these were to her the most precious opportunities of showing her love to her Heavenly Father. But far more important than these details in her relations to things was her relation to other souls. In every one of her sisters in religion she saw another child of her heavenly Father, who was to be loved. This vision inspired her to a life of wonderful devotion to them in little things. It was this simple, childlike approach to everything which made her able to give the smallest things a supernatural value. For example: in the laundry, while they were doing their washing, the nun opposite her splashed her unnecessarily. Instead of being resentful, St Thérèse welcomed it as little gift she could offer to her Heavenly Father.

On another occasion, in the chapel, she found herself next to an old sister who unceasingly rattled her beads and made other noises which distracted her. Her first reaction was to turn round and give her a look that would make her stop. Instead she said to herself: "Here is just a little opportunity to bearing with one of my sisters". And she set herself to listening to what she now called "the music", and offered it to her Heavenly Father. One of the old sisters, being infirm, had to be led to the refectory every evening. She was extremely difficult to deal with, never being satisfied with the way things were done for her. In undertaking this little service, Thérèse succeeded where all others had failed, because of the childlike tenderness which she bestowed upon her, finishing her task every evening with a smile of such sweetness that the old sister was charmed. Another time it would be a sister who had, as St Thérèse says herself, the capacity for annoying and irritating her in every single thing she did. When she met her in the cloister her first instinct was to avoid her and go round by the other way. But once again her simple, childlike love conquered. Abandoning herself to her Father's care, she set herself to do everything she could for this sister, helping her in every possible way, till at last the sister turned to her and said: "Sister Thérèse, what is it you see in me that attracts you so?"

Sometimes this love would show a sterner side: as when she would pass along the cloister in silence and refuse to speak to nuns older than herself who were talking and thus breaking their rule. For a child of sixteen to act thus was little less than heroism, and only a very humble abandonment to the power of her Father's love could have made it possible.

Much of what we have been considering will of course appear trivial. Why make such a fuss over little things? And here we face the whole point. It is precisely this self-conquest, for it is nothing less than self-conquest, in little things which the world never realises, which is the real secret of sanctity in great things. We shall see this as we go on. But it is good to pause for a moment to dispose of this specious but entirely worldly objection to her type of sanctity.

Before we go on to the sterner proofs of her love for God and for her sisters, it would be good to understand how it influenced her prayer. In this she was, above all else, her Father's little child. Apart from the Divine Office and the Liturgy she did not use long prayers. To her, prayer was a very simple thing. The lifting of the mind, a cry, a simple glance towards her Heavenly Father – that, to her, was enough. This she was doing all day long: not asking her Heavenly Father to do what she

wanted, but simply asking Him from moment to moment
to show her what He wanted her to be and to do. This
simple prayer was in fact a continual conscious surrender
of her will to her Heavenly Father's; that is to say,
humbling herself to utter nothingness so that He could
carry her in His arms through difficult situations, amid
darkness, up to heights of sacrifice which, by herself, she
could never have attained. In this prayer, if she should
fall asleep she did not worry, knowing that a father could
never be angry with his child when it falls asleep, weary
through loving him. Thus in her prayer – and it is on our
prayer that all our supernatural life and action depend –
she was saved from all morbid and dangerous scruples.

That her love was neither weak nor sentimental is shown
by the fact that it resulted in complete obliteration of herself
in the service of God and the Community. She prayed at her
Profession that she might be forgotten by all, trodden
underfoot like a little grain of sand. To the world this again
sounds morbid, because the world cannot see that she desired
to be trodden under foot in order that she might be free from
any self-love, any desire for flattery or recognition, and so be
able to rise to loving God and those around her, unfettered by
such human weakness. Thus she specially preferred doing
things for others that were never known, watching for any
little thing that had been left undone or needed to be done
that had not been noticed, rejoicing to be able to do
something for others that was never known and never seen.

One of the results of this was that, at the time of her death, a lay sister was heard speaking about her thus: "Sister Thérèse will soon die and I cannot help asking myself what our Mother will have to say about her after her death, for this little sister, amiable though she is, has surely done nothing worth recording". This obliteration of herself was shown in various ways. In the refectory she concealed her tastes so well that the cook used to say when there was anything left over, "Sister Thérèse will eat it".

This desire to be forgotten she presses to its logical conclusion even in her prayer. Not content with being misunderstood, unappreciated, forgotten by her sisters, she was willing to be apparently forgotten by God. In her spiritual life, in which she was almost invariably without consolation, she remained so perfectly the confident child of her Heavenly Father, so completely abandoned to His love, so completely resting in His arms, that she never desired to see His face: content, as she said, to hide her face in His bosom, and in this hiddenness and darkness finding just that particular joy which only the Night of Faith can give to souls, that particular supernatural apprehension of the unseen world which only comes by Faith and not by feeling. She was thus proof against all despair and all disappointment.

This is the secret of that heroic virtue which, in secret, was growing steadily in the life of this wonderful saint.

There was however one member at least of the Community from whom this hidden sanctity of the little

Saint could not remain entirely concealed. That person was Mother Agnes. On being made Prioress in February, 1893, she appointed St Thérèse to assist the novice mistress in the training of the novices. This post she retained for the remaining four years of her life. During this time she chose to remain within the novitiate, though entitled to rank among the professed nuns of the Community. Such an admirable example of humility could not but influence the souls under her care. The record of her conversations and dealing with the novices towards the end was carefully preserved, for the nuns realised that this precious life was drawing to its close. It forms a complete treatise in itself: a treatise showing her prudence, acute judgment of character, unerring tactfulness, tenderness, and strength in exquisite proportion, and above all a complete disinterestedness in the handling of those under her. Were it not for this record we should be very much the poorer for we should have been without one of the most fruitful sources of our knowledge of the wonderful dealings of God's grace in this chosen soul.

One winter's evening, December, 1894, little Thérèse in recreation was recounting some of the memories of her childhood to her Sister Marie and Mother Agnes, then Prioress. After recreation was over Marie begged Mother Agnes to tell Thérèse to put into writing some of these memories, so convinced was she of their value. For some time Mother Agnes hesitated, finally she directed the

Saint to do so under obedience. Thérèse obeyed, though in her heart she was a little fearful and reluctant. She could only give it her leisure moments, which were not many, as her work in the Sacristy often encroached on her free time. She began it early in 1895 and finished it by 20th January 1896.

On entering choir for evening prayer, she approached the Prioress and, kneeling, gave her the manuscript, written without any erasure, during her odd moments, in a little twopenny copybook. Mother Agnes acknowledged it with a nod of the head, put it in her stall and forgot about it till some months after. All this time St Thérèse was quite unconcerned and never mentioned the matter, and showed no sign of surprise when one day Mother Agnes remarked that she had not yet read it. Later on, when relieved of the office of Prioress and having more leisure, Mother Agnes read the manuscript, she at once realised the value of these pages, and urged Mother Gonzaga to tell the Saint under obedience to continue the story of her life in the convent. And so were added Chapters IX and X to the first eight chapters of the autobiography. Other supplementary pages were added on her doctrine of the Little Way and addressed to her sister Marie. And so almost haphazardly the autobiography, which is now famous throughout the world, came into being.

One external mark of St Thérèse's inner strength was her physical endurance. So bright was she, so continual was her smile, so unfailing her readiness to help in anything that was needed, that no one suspected that there was anything wrong with her physical health. Beyond a little pallor from time to time, and certain signs of weariness inevitable in the Carmelite life, they could see nothing to cause anxiety. But, in spite of this, unknown to those around her, the rigours of the Carmelite life had begun to tell their tale: the fasts, the long hours of prayer, the continual manual work, had taken their toll. In the winter the cold caused her intense suffering. There was just one fire at which it was possible to warm herself before retiring to her cell. This fire was a small one, and she had to cross the open cloister afterwards to reach her cell. She was cold through and through before she got to bed, and for long intervals had practically no sleep, lying awake because of the cold which penetrated her whole being. The fact that she felt the cold to this degree only came out when, towards the end of her life, she was told under obedience to say what had tried her most.

Not long after her Profession the convent was invaded by the scourge of influenza which at that time spread over Europe. At one stage Sister Thérèse and one other sister were the only two who were not laid up. Upon them fell the entire work of nursing their sisters, and of attending to all the needs of the convent and chapel. Sister Thérèse herself caught the infection and was considered to have had it very slightly. Most probably, with her usual courage, she concealed her illness from the others, for it was her principle "to go to the furthest limits of endurance rather than complain". At all events, she was in the midst of it all, as we have said, nursing the sick and doing the work of the convent. Night after night she was up, attending to the dying. At one time she tells how she had closed the eyes of one sister when she became conscious that another had also passed to her reward. All alone she had to perform the last offices, for there was literally nobody to assist her. This little picture will give us some idea of the self-effacing courage with which she, only just recovered, spent her strength in the service of others.

All this took its toll on the young Saint and her health began to fail.

Last Illness

The Heavenly Father is now about to lead His little child through the valley of the shadow of death.

The remaining eighteen months of the Saint's life form the story of how, with invincible love, profound humility, and the complete abandonment of a little child, she surrenders herself to that Heavenly Father's love: how, safe in her Father's arms, she moves along the road of physical pain and spiritual desolation: and how at last, through death, she passes to that final embrace which is Heaven itself.

We will now watch her as she passes through her hour of trial.

The first definite warning came on the early morning of Good Friday, 3rd April 1896. She tells the story with the calm simplicity so characteristic of her.

"At midnight I returned to our cell. Scarcely was my head laid on the pillow when I felt a hot stream rise to my lips. I thought I was going to die and my heart nearly broke with joy. But, as I had already put out my lamp, I mortified my curiosity until the morning and slept in peace. At five o'clock, when it was time to get up, I remembered at once that I had some good news to learn; and, going to the window, I found, as I had expected, my handkerchief soaked with blood". She came down to chapel for the morning prayers as usual, and afterwards told the Mother Prioress what had happened. But she made so light of it that she was given permission to continue the ordinary life of the Carmel as usual. It was not till a few months later that a hard, dry cough, which she could not hide, made the fact that she was ill evident to all.

Along with all this physical suffering her Heavenly Father, in His Providence, sent her a far greater trial. From henceforth she was to pass through a time of continual temptations against the Faith, temptations which were not to cease till the moment of her death. She describes this desolation as a great wall raised between her and heaven, shutting out the very stars. She tells how an interior voice was continually telling her that there was nothing after death and that all her life of sacrifice and all her hopes were vain.

The thought of heaven which always had been to her a thing of joy, became now the subject of intense torture. To quote her own words: "When my heart, weary of the surrounding darkness, tries to find some rest in the thought of a life to come, my anguish increases. It seems to me that out of the darkness I hear the mocking voice of the unbeliever: 'You dream of a land of light and fragrance; you dream that the Creator of these wonders shall be yours for ever. You think one day to escape from these mists wherein you now languish. Nay, rejoice in death, which will give you not what you hope for, but a night darker still, the night of utter nothingness'... May God forgive me; He knows that I try to live by Faith though it does not afford me the least consolation. I have made more acts of Faith in this last year than during all the rest of my life".

Once or twice during this period a flash of light was allowed to illuminate the darkness, only to leave a darkness even darker still. One of these was an incident in the garden of the Carmel where, towards the end of her illness, she was walking, supported by her sister, Mother Agnes. While so doing she saw a little white hen gathering her chickens under her wing. The Saint asked her sister to take her back to her cell, and when they reached it she was in tears. When Mother Agnes asked her the reason of her tears she replied: "Did you not see that mother-hen with her chickens? Well, that is exactly what God had done with me all my life. He has entirely hidden me under the shadow of His wings. I am thankful He does not let me see it often as I saw it just now, for I could not bear it".

Apart from these rare occasions all was darkness within and pain without. The illness made rapid progress, developing into intestinal tuberculosis. In his efforts to prevent a recurrence of haemorrhage, the doctor subjected her to a further and painful course of treatment by blisterings and cauterisations. Ever smiling and with gentle words of gratitude, the sufferer endured these remedies, which at that time were more painful than the illness itself.

For a few months she got better; and such was her invincible courage that she at once regained her hope of being allowed to go to the convent of Hanoi at Tonkin in Indo-China, where they were asking for her. For thus she desired to show her love for her Lord by dying in the mission field, as it were in exile, in a convent where she would be utterly unknown. She began a novena for this purpose, but scarcely was it over when a grave relapse supervened. All through the winter her strength gradually declined. Towards Lent in 1897 very alarming symptoms declared themselves. The doctor continued his severe remedies, though with little hope of recovery. After each treatment the Saint had to remain very quiet for several hours.

Throughout all this time of suffering she possessed a calmness which came from a source little known to the world. Mother Agnes entered her cell one evening and said to her: "Why are you so joyful today?" Thérèse replied: "Because I have had this morning two little trials – and very painful they were – and nothing gives me little joys so much as little trials".

The secret of this joy lay in the fact that she had learnt to turn her suffering to such practical account. She was ordered to take exercise for a quarter of an hour a day to enjoy the warm sunshine of the spring. A sister, seeing her walking with great difficulty, said: "You ought to be in bed, not walking like this". "Perhaps", said the Saint, "but you know what gives me strength? I offer each step for a missionary. I recollect that in a distant land one of them is perhaps worn out by his labours. To lessen his fatigue I offer mine to God".

Thinking that the end was not far off, she took advantage of the presence of her three sisters in her cell to bid them farewell. In so doing she said to them: "Do not be astonished that I do not appear to you after my death, and that you do not see anything extraordinary that would make my happiness known to you. Remember, that it is my little way to desire nothing of that kind". (In point of fact she never has appeared to any of them.) She then added: "I would like, however, to have an easy death in order to console you, but do not be disturbed if I suffer greatly and if you cannot see any signs of happiness at the moment of my death. Our Saviour was truly a victim of love and see how great was His agony! The death of love which I so much desire is that of Jesus on the Cross".

Fearing another haemorrhage, they thought it best to take her from her cell to the Infirmary. On leaving her cell, she said to her sister: "I wish so much I could have died there. This little cell is so precious to me, for I have had the joy of suffering so much there". On arriving in the infirmary her eyes fell on the statue of Our Lady. "Why are you looking at her?" asked her sister. She answered: "I have never seen her looking so beautiful as she is today. Today it is the statue that is beautiful; but that other day, when she smiled at me, as you well know, it was not the statue but it was herself". So the Blessed Mother who had come to her succour in her first illness was to be her companion in her last.

It was at about this point in her illness that she began to speak about herself and her future in a way which can only be explained as inspired by God. One day her sister Marie said to her, "What a sorrow it will be for us when you die!" "Oh no," she replied joyously, "you will see, after my death, I will let fall a shower of roses". To Mother Agnes, speaking in the same strain, she said, "You will not have time to miss me, the postman will keep you so busy on my account". On 16th July, Thérèse made another prophetic announcement which has now become famous throughout the world. She turned to Mother Agnes and said: "I feel that my mission is soon to begin, my mission to teach souls my little way... Yes... I will spend my heaven in doing good upon earth". "What is this little way which you would teach to souls?" "It is", she replied, "the way of spiritual childhood, the way of trust and absolute self-surrender". A few days later, when in conversation with her, her sisters said: "You will look down on us from Heaven". She answered: "No, I will come down and I will help priests, missionaries, and the whole Church". Thus on her dying bed she expresses that thirst for souls by which she had been possessed ever since that moment when, as a child, she had seen the picture of her crucified Saviour slip from her book at Mass.

On 1st August, just two months before she died, Mother Agnes told the Saint that she intended to have the account of her life, which, under obedience, she had written, published after her death, but that she feared there would be opposition. The Saint replied simply and without hesitation: "Mother, after my death my manuscript should not be spoken of to anyone until it is published. If you do otherwise or delay the publication, the devil will set many snares for you in order to hinder God's good work – a work that is very important". Her counsel was followed. Having obtained the imprimatur of the Bishop on 8th March 1898, the autobiography appeared during the October following. A few weeks later, by reason of newly arisen circumstances, its publication would have been impossible. One day Mother Agnes gave the manuscript to little Thérèse, asking her to revise a passage which seemed to her incomplete.

Entering the infirmary soon afterwards she saw that the Saint's eyes were filled with tears. She asked her why? Thérèse replied with an indefinable expression: "It is indeed the manifestation of my soul. Yes, these pages will do a great deal of good. Through them God's gentleness and sweetness will become better known". And she added in an inspired tone: "Yes, I know it, everyone will love me". In view of what has happened since it is impossible to deny the Saint's gift of prophecy.

Haemorrhages of a more serious nature than ever took place during the last days of July, so that it was thought wise to administer the Last Sacraments. Before the Extreme Unction she asked pardon of all the Community in such a touching manner that many of the sisters could not refrain their tears. Then with a radiant smile she said: "The door of my dark prison is now half open".

Last Months

It was expected that she would soon pass from this world; but in reality a martyrdom of two long months was just beginning.

One night she begged the sister who was attending her to sprinkle holy water on the bed, saying: "The devil is near me; I do not see him, but I feel his presence. He torments me; he holds me with a hand of iron, preventing me from getting the slightest relief; he increases my pain in order to lead me to despair. I cannot pray. I can only look at the Blessed Virgin and say 'Jesus'. How necessary is that prayer at Compline: 'Deliver us from the phantoms of the night'. I experience something mysterious; I do not suffer for myself but for another soul... and the devil is angry".

From 17th Augusth vomiting became so frequent that it was impossible to give her Communion any longer. This was the most cruel trial of all. At the same time her physical sufferings kept increasing so that even the doctor himself was driven to exclaim: "Ah, if only you knew what this young nun is suffering! Never have I seen such suffering borne with such supernatural joy".

How did she meet this acute physical suffering, and this deep spiritual desolation? Mother Agnes said to her one morning: "Your sufferings are terrible"; to which she replied: "No, they are not terrible; how can a victim of love find anything terrible that is sent her by her Spouse? At each moment He sends me what I am able to bear; nothing more. And if He increases my pain, He increases my strength as well. But I can never ask for greater sufferings: I am too little a soul, for then they would be my own choice and I should have to bear them without His help, and I have never been able to do anything when left to myself". Here then is the answer: she was such a child, so little, that she let her Heavenly Father take her in His Arms and carry her through it all. Her littleness is the secret of her fortitude; more than this, with inexorable logic, she presses her philosophy of a little child to its very end. Why does an earthly father hide himself from his little one? Only that the little one may seek him all the more. And if the distress of the little one grows too great, he leaves his hiding place and shows himself, and all is well. We grown-ups call it hide-and-seek. Little Thérèse on her dying bed turned her darkness and desolation into a game of hide-and-seek with her Heavenly Father. Listen to her triumphant words: "He will get tired of making me wait sooner than I shall get tired of waiting". This is how she met it: this is heroic sanctity indeed. Even more, it was of these trials that she made her Heaven on Earth. She sings of this Heaven in one of her poems:

> *"My Heaven is to smile on the God whom I adore,*
> *Whene'er He wills to hide Himself to prove my faith:*
> *To smile, the while awaiting till*
> *He looks on me once more,*
> *That! That is Heaven to me".*

It was impossible that one so human and so sensitive to human frailty should not taste the natural shrinking from death. On 11th September she said: "I am afraid that I have had the fear of death, but I have not had the fear of what will follow after my death. I only say to myself: 'What is this mysterious separation of soul and body?' It is the first time I have experienced that feeling, but I immediately abandon myself to God". And she added at once: "Please give me the crucifix that I may kiss it in order to gain the indulgence for the souls in Purgatory. This is all I can do for them now".

One of her sisters asked if she would be afraid of death. "That may easily come to pass", she replied. "I do not rely on my own feelings, for I know my own frailty, but I wish to enjoy all the peace God gives me now. It will be time to bear that cross when it comes". Through all this her love for her Heavenly Father and her confidence in Him remained invincible and serene. "How happy I am to die", she writes a month before her death, "happy because in Heaven far more than here I shall be able to help the souls I love". Just as to Our Blessed Lord His Passion was the precious gift of the Father to the Son: "The chalice that my Father has given me, shall I not drink it?" – so to little Thérèse her sufferings were her Heavenly Father's most precious gift to her, His little child. To kiss her crucifix, that little crucifix with its Figure worn by her caresses, was one of the Saint's principal manifestations of love during these days of suffering.

On 14th September a rose was brought to her. Taking its petals, she tenderly touched with each one the wounds of her dying Saviour. Some of the petals fell from her bed to the floor; and she said to her sisters: "Gather up these petals. Do not lose one of them. Later on you will need them". In point of fact, in September 1910, one of these petals cured a man, Ferdinand Aubry, of Lisieux, of cancer of the tongue.

On one of her last nights on earth, her sister Céline, Sister Geneviève, entered the infirmary and found her with hands joined and eyes raised to Heaven. "What are you doing?" she said, "you should try to get a little sleep". "I cannot sleep", Thérèse replied, "I am praying". "And what are you asking of Jesus?" "I cannot say anything: I just love Him". The same sister found her on another occasion with the crucifix in her hand, passing her fingers tenderly over the wounded brow and mangled limbs of her Saviour. When asked what she was doing she answered: "I am taking out the nails, and raising from His brow the crown of thorns".

From 25th September she was so weak that she could no longer make the least movement unaided. The sound of voices, even in low tones, near her bed became a torment to her. In the burning heat of fever, and with a terrible sense of suffocation, she could not speak a word without acute pain. To her great delight a little robin used to come and perch on the window-sill and, entering the sickroom, used to flit about her bed. The evening before her death, at about nine o'clock, a sound of fluttering wings was heard in the garden, and a turtle-dove (no one knew where it came from) alighted on the window-sill and for a long time stayed there, softly cooing. Little Thérèse and her sister Céline recalled the words: "The song of the turtle is heard in our land... Arise, my love, my dove, and come, for winter is now past".

Early on the morning of 29th September a distressing rattle in the throat seemed to announce the end. Towards noon, the little sufferer turned to the Prioress, Mother Mary Gonzaga: "Is it today, Mother?" she asked. "Yes", the Prioress replied. Some hours later she was heard to murmur: "I am utterly exhausted: I can do no more. Oh, pray for me.... if you only knew!" Her sister Céline, bending over her, asked for a last message. Speaking with great difficulty and very faintly, the little Saint replied: "It is love alone that counts". She lingered on during another night. In the morning, casting a glance on the statue of the Blessed Virgin which was facing her bed, she said: "Oh, with what fervour I have prayed to her, but it was pure agony without any consolation. Earth's air is stifling me; when shall I breathe the air of Heaven?"

All day the fever consumed her. "Ah", she said, "if this is the agony, what then is death?" Then again, addressing the Prioress, she said: "Oh, Mother, I assure you that the chalice is full to the brim. My God, Thou art so good!" Towards three o'clock she stretched her arms in the form of a cross. Mother Mary Gonzaga placed on her knees the image of Our Lady of Mount Carmel. "Oh, Mother", she said, "present me to the Blessed Virgin without delay. Prepare me to die well". The Prioress reminded her that, as she had always understood the practised humility, she could count on receiving mercy. Little Thérèse thought for a moment and then replied: "Yes, I have understood humility of heart". Then, in tones of deep conviction: "All that I have written of my desire for suffering is really true. I do not repent of having surrendered myself to love".

A few hours later she was heard to murmur: "I would never have believed that it was possible to suffer so much, never, never! I can only explain it by my intense desire to save souls".

Towards five o'clock Mother Agnes, who was alone with her, noticed a sudden change. This time it was indeed the death agony. A hurried summons of the bell called the Community to the infirmary. The little Saint had a smile for each of the sisters, then she became absorbed in the contemplation of her crucifix. For two hours the struggle continued. To cool the fever that was burning her lips, her sister Céline bent down and refreshed them with a small particle of ice. A look of infinite tenderness and a sweet smile of gratitude rewarded the "little companion of her childhood" for this last act of love.

Towards seven o'clock, as the sufferer seemed to grow no worse, the Mother Prioress dismissed the Community. Turning towards her, the dying Saint murmured: "Has the agony not come yet, Mother? Am I not going to die?"

"Yes, my child, this is the agony; but God wishes perhaps to prolong it for a few hours". "Well then", she murmured, "Let it be so. Oh, I would not wish to suffer less!" Then, fixing her eyes on the crucifix: "Oh", she murmured, "I love Him. My God, I... Love... Thee..." These were her last words. Slowly she fell back on the pillow, and then, suddenly raising herself up as if called by a mysterious voice, she opened her eyes, which shone with a peace and joy beyond all words to describe; and, with a look of surprised wonder and radiant happiness, she surrendered her soul into her Heavenly Father's Arms, to the end His little child.

IN HEAVEN

Thus, hidden in the obscurity of Carmel, Thérèse died. Four days after, on 4th October 1897, the doors of Carmel were thrown open, and her worn-out body was carried across the threshold over which, a short nine years before, she had passed as a girl of fifteen. Out of the Carmel chapel, where she had knelt as a little girl with her father and for the first time had heard the voices of the nuns at prayer, they passed into the street and made their way to the cemetery. This little procession was typical of Thérèse, who loved always to be hidden and forgotten. It consisted of a mere handful of relations and friends following the simple coffin which rested on the common bier used for the funerals of the poor. Led by the priest, they made their way up the hill and along the winding lane. The coffin was lowered into the grave, the earth thrown in; the few mourners then withdrew, thinking that the little sister's work on earth was over. Humanly speaking it was the end. How could it be otherwise? for she had done nothing that could bring any earthly glory.

One thing only might lead us to expect that all was not ended here – her own words: "I will spend my Heaven doing good on earth"; and this was but one of many such prophecies which she had made when she was ill.

Were these sayings misguided boastings, the delusions of a mind weakened by sickness? Or were they the voice of God speaking through His child? If they were of God, only God could vindicate them; for, humanly speaking, it was utterly impossible that they should be fulfilled. Let us watch the facts as they develop.

The Autobiography

It is the custom of Carmel on the death of one of the Community to publish a short account of the sister's life and doings and to send it to the other Carmels. In this case it was decided that the account of her life which Thérèse herself had written should serve this purpose.

The book appeared during the October of 1898, just a year after her death. The first edition consisted of two thousand copies. On hearing of this, one of the nuns remarked: "Whatever shall we do with these? We shall surely have them left on our hands".

From the first however the book met with an enthusiastic reception. In convent after convent it was read with eagerness, and from the convents it was lent to friends. Everywhere souls were stirred. In many cases those who had left the Church came back after reading it. The first edition was rapidly exhausted. Before the Canonisation the circulation of this book had reached the amazing figure of 410,000. In 1932 it had risen to 700,675; while the shorter Life – the abridged edition – had reached nothing less than

2,321,000. Altogether it has been translated into thirty-five languages or dialects; and constantly new versions are being asked for: all this without any efforts on the part of Carmel, which has contented itself with merely authorising these versions when submitted to them.

Today there is no part of the Catholic Church, no country, no mission, where this book is not loved and read. It carries with it a supernatural power almost unparalleled.

The Holy Father, speaking to all the faithful, says: "The book on her own life, written by Sister Thérèse in the limpid beauty of her mother-tongue, in order to make known her Way of Spiritual Childhood, is not only in the hands of all, but its sweetness penetrates the hearts of men most estranged from Christian perfection. Numbers of them have been converted by reading it and are now firmly rooted in the Charity of Christ".

And this is that little book which was written at odd moments, amid continual distractions, during exhausting illness, without any effort after literary style; written in a poor little copybook; the book which was put on one side for months and forgotten; the book the value of which she herself only realised at the very last when she said: "This work is very important. These pages will do a great deal of good".

The Shower of Roses

Wherever the Autobiography was read and to whatever part of the world it penetrated, the immediate result was that those who read it appealed to little Thérèse for her supernatural aid; confiding to her their troubles, seeking her consolation in their sorrows, asking her for relief in sickness or for patience in their pain and often for a happy death.

The result was overwhelming. From every part of the world came reports of miracles of physical healing and, more important, miracles of supernatural grace. Men and women were not merely restored to bodily health but brought back to their faith and to the Church. Missions that had long been languishing sprang to life. Districts in the mission field where there had been no conversions for years were suddenly overwhelmed by people asking to be baptised and taught. Her help extended to every rank of society, but she seemed to have a special love for the poor and humble, the sick and the abandoned, and especially for little children. Above all her help was lavished upon priests. On every side priests were strengthened in their labours, consoled in their loneliness, comforted in their sickness. All who committed their ministry to her care had the same story to tell of wonders happening which they could not account for on any other basis than that they were her answer to their prayers. Taking her as his model, many a priest who had lost heart and grown lukewarm found his early aspirations rekindled and his soul set on fire again with the Love of God. "Pray to her", said Pope Benedict XV to a priest, "it is her vocation to teach priests how to love Jesus Christ".

This shower of roses – these miracles and favours – became so numerous that it was utterly impossible to note them all. Such as were recorded have been gathered together and can be read in seven volumes comprising no less than 4,800 pages of close type which have already reached the phenomenal circulation of 198,000 copies. Yet this account presents only a small fraction of the miracles: for until the year 1902, so far from any accurate record being kept, we have hardly any records at all, for thousands of letters received by Carmel during those years were destroyed.

The pages of those seven volumes are the record of her ministry amid the most poignant of human misery in all its varied forms. To love, to be loved, and to return to earth to make Love loved had been Thérèse's great desire. These miracles are that desire's fulfilment. The late Pope, Pius XI, pointed this out. "We have proof that on entering Paradise she began at once this work among souls when we see the mystical shower of roses which God permitted and still permits her to let fall on earth, as she had ingenuously foretold". And again: "We earnestly desire that all the faithful in Christ should prove themselves worthy of this abundant outpouring of grace, this mystical shower of roses which St Thérèse of the Child Jesus scatters without ceasing." No wonder that the Holy Father called her "a prodigy of miracles".

As a result of this shower of roses came the immense flood of letters with which Carmel was inundated. The post soon became unmanageable. By the year 1911 it had reached the figure of a hundred letters a day, while in 1923, before her canonisation, the daily number had risen to five hundred. By the 1930s, if we include all the various departments at Lisieux, it surpassed a thousand a day. To deal with it, more than fifty secretaries were required. Indeed her little mother, Mother Agnes, was, as the Saint foretold, kept too busy to feel her loss. This post was sometimes very embarrassing, for the power of the little Saint penetrates to such unknown regions that some of the letters were in languages which nobody at Lisieux could decipher.

A World-Wide Devotion

In response to the shower of roses and to the love which the Saint lavished throughout the world, it is not surprising that there sprang up a devotion phenomenal in the rapidity of its growth and in its world-wide appeal.

Foremost, in expressing this devotion was Pope Pius XI. To her he turned in his many difficulties. He called her "the beloved star of his pontificate", his "consoling angel in all his trials". Her statue was on his writing table, immediately before his eyes; and, in his free moments, he was frequently found on his knees before a statue of her which he himself caused to be erected in the garden of the Vatican City. To the bishops who came to see him he did not hesitate to say: "Pray to St Thérèse of the Child Jesus. We invoke her ceaselessly. Go and visit her sanctuary at Lisieux".

There is not a country in Europe where souls do not come under her sway. France naturally takes the lead in this devotion with nearly a hundred sanctuaries dedicated to her name. In Belgium and Italy the story is the same. In Eastern Europe and throughout most of Western Europe, her name is loved and reverenced. More extraordinary still, she casts her spell over many outside the Catholic Church. The power of her appeal is felt among the Orthodox in Eastern Europe, the Protestant churches and even among Muslims. If we pass to America we find a devotion quite extraordinary. Here the devotion has resulted in more frequent Communions and greater earnestness in the reception of the Sacraments. She challenges the materialism of that great nation by the simplicity of her appeal. In Mexico, in South America – Brazil, Argentina, Chile – everywhere St Thérèse is known and loved, and churches and sanctuaries rise in her honour.

But perhaps the most remarkable response of all is seen in the mission field. Throughout Africa, India, China, the story is the same. She transcends all nationality; all differences of colour disappear. The same homage is given her by them all. From Morocco to Natal, from Dahomey to Abyssinia, the "White Virgin of France" is revered and loved. In Uganda a great hospital was dedicated to her. In Madagascar and in the immense regions of the Congo, churches are ever being consecrated to her name; missions are placed under her protection; seminaries take her as the

model for their students. Even her poems, translated into
the language of the land, are seen in these far-flung
frontiers of the Church. It was this universal and
unprecedented devotion which led the Holy Father to
declare her officially Patroness of the Missions and to
describe her publicly as "the child loved by all the world".

The Pilgrimage to Lisieux

Not content with invoking the aid of the Saint in their
homes the faithful soon began to find their way to Lisieux
to pray to her at her very shrine. Individuals began to do
so from the very first. Soon individuals became groups,
hundreds became thousands, till by 1923 they numbered
fifty thousand a year. Thus this grave, indistinguishable in
its simplicity from other graves around, became a shrine
for all the world, and this while the Church had not yet
spoken and she was still the simple Sister Thérèse of the
Child Jesus. Later, in 1925, the number rose to 310,000.
During the years before the Church had spoken, no fewer
than four of the College of Cardinals found their way to
seek the aid of the little Saint in their arduous duties. Of
these one was Cardinal Bourne, Archbishop of
Westminster, who visited the grave in 1919. In this
stream of pilgrims were numberless bishops, while priests
and missionaries came in thousands. Mingling with them
were men and women drawn from every station in life
and from every country in the world. It was life with all

its hopes and fears, sorrows and joys, failures and successes, life with all its essential tragedy, that was to be seen month after month, year after year, seeking this hitherto almost unknown town of Normandy.

In 1914 there broke upon France the Great War, engulfing all Europe in its horror. And now Lisieux and the grave of the little Saint became the scene of another human stream mingling with the first – a stream of soldiers, officers, and men, of widows and orphaned children, of the wounded – all the wreckage the War brought in its train. Miraculously preserved by St Thérèse in the trenches, soldiers came to offer her their thanks and their homage. And once again they came in thousands. It was the innumerable letters from the trenches, appealing for her canonisation, which so profoundly moved the Vatican that Benedict XV, as early as 1915, took the unusual course of authorising that a medal should be struck for the soldiers in honour of St Thérèse.

The Canonisation

Profoundly moved by the innumerable miracles, impressed and urged by the appeals of the faithful from every quarter of the world, the Holy See thought fit in 1910 to begin the process of Canonisation. In that year the first enquiry into her writings, her life, and her virtues was held at Bayeaux. On 10th June Pius X signed the decree for the introduction of her cause. This cause was destined to go forward with a rapidity literally unparalleled. Benedict XV, in order to hasten the process, dispensed with the fifty years which Canon Law demands should intervene between death and beatification; and on 14th August 1921, the same Holy Father signed the decree affirming that "the servant of God had practised virtue to an heroic degree". In this decree he declared that "in Spiritual Childhood lies the secret of sanctity for all the faithful". When he died the following January he left to his successor, Pope Pius XI, the continuation of the cause. This Holy Father was to have the unique experience that the first saint to be beatified by him should also be the first to be canonised during his pontificate.

The securing of the two miracles necessary for Beatification was easy. But before Beatification could take place it was necessary that the venerated remains of little Thérèse should be taken from the cemetery to the Carmel and identified with solemn ceremony. The date fixed for this was 26th March 1923. That morning over fifty thousand pilgrims arrived in the town of Lisieux. Patiently they waited while the work of exhuming the precious coffin was proceeding. As the coffin was being lifted from the grave the scent of roses came from the tomb and was noticed by all of those standing near. The coffin was placed on a carriage draped in white. Escorted by more than two hundred priests, by the dignitaries of the town and by thousands of the faithful, the precious relics of little Thérèse were carried, this time in triumph, along the road to her convent. The immense procession was an imposing sight. Not a hymn, not a note of music, broke the stillness, for the laws of the Church forbade any manifestation resembling a religious cult until Rome had given her official decision. The only sound that broke the silence was the murmuring of the Rosary by the faithful. On the journey down to Carmel, as the coffin was carried by, a wounded soldier, who had lost the use of his legs, recovered suddenly and completely, while the eyes of a girl who was blind were opened to behold the holy relics arrive at the Carmel gate. These were but two of the wonders that happened that day. So once more the earthly remains of little Thérèse were carried across the threshold of Carmel, to be received by her three sisters, who had parted from them with such sorrow only twenty-six years before.

What a contrast between that little company of friends and relatives which on 4th October 1897, followed the unknown Carmelite to her grave and this triumphal procession that twenty-six years later brought her back to her convent amid the fervent joy of devoted thousands.

On April 29th 1923, Thérèse's beatitude in the glory of Heaven was proclaimed by the Head of the Church. In the splendidly decorated basilica of St Peter, in the presence of forty-five archbishops and bishops, together with a vast concourse of the faithful, the pontifical brief was read.

The burden of it was the Little Way of Spiritual Childhood, of which St Thérèse was proclaimed to all the faithful as the teacher. Wonderful as this was, we must not pause here, for greater glories were yet to come.

The unanimous veneration coming successively from every continent was to Rome, as it were, an international plebiscite, demanding that the Holy Father should officially proclaim Thérèse to be a saint of the Catholic Church. This unanimous voice of the people, together with the evidence of miracles, brought Pius XI to an immediate decision. Once more the canonical statutes appointing a long delay between beatification and canonisation must yield, he said, "to the supplication of the whole Catholic world". Twenty-eight years after her death, two years after her beatification, while yet her four sisters were living, little Thérèse, the little flower of Les Buissonnets, the strong saint of Carmel, the untiring strewer of roses, the providential helper of the outcast, the poor, and the suffering, was, to the indescribable joy of the whole Catholic world, to become St Thérèse of the Child Jesus.

The day chosen for this great triumph was 17th May 1925. The scene in St Peter's baffles description. Never had such an assembly gathered at any canonisation as this, it was probably the largest and most distinguished gathering that had been seen beneath the dome of Michaelangelo for centuries. Thirty-four cardinals were present. Over two hundred archbishops and bishops followed in the procession. Innumerable prelates, representatives of the religious orders, priests, and missionaries in their hundreds walked behind them. When they had passed to their seats, there came the splendid banner with the picture of the Saint. Then came the entry of the Holy Father. Slowly, in the midst of this magnificent throng, he was borne to the splendid throne erected in front of St Peter's chair.

The moment had come to declare solemnly before the whole Church the entry of little Thérèse into the glory of Heaven. The invocation of the Holy Ghost was repeated; and then came the solemn words: "Arise, Peter is about to speak by the mouth of Pius". A tense silence held captive that tremendous throng. Seated on the chair of Peter, Pius XI, his face radiant with joy, pronounced the formula which was to send heavenwards a fervent Hosanna from the Universal Church: "We declare Blessed Thérèse of the Child Jesus to be a Saint. We define that such she is... In the Name of the Father and of the Son and of the Holy Ghost. Amen." The infallible teacher had spoken. Immediately there burst forth the exultant tones of the silver trumpets. The bells of St Peter's pealed, and with their deep notes were mingled those of the bells of every church in the Eternal City. The acclamations of the thousands in the basilica swelled into one great thunder of applause which was taken up by the two hundred thousand waiting in the square outside. Never had there been such a canonisation as this.

After the Gospel, the Holy Father pointed out to the whole Catholic Church the reason of this canonisation. It was in order to exalt St Thérèse before the whole world as the teacher of the Little Way of Spiritual Childhood. His homily ended with the ringing words: "We desire most earnestly that all the faithful should study her in order to copy her, becoming children themselves, since otherwise they cannot, according to the word of the Master, arrive at the Kingdom of Heaven. If this Way of Spiritual Childhood were to be universally followed, who can fail to see how easily would be realised that reformation of human society which We set ourselves to accomplish at the commencement of Our pontificate?"

Here then, in the basilica of St Peter's, in a scene of unparalleled splendour, through the mouth of the Supreme Head of the Church on earth speaking to all the faithful, is the fulfilment of those simple words, spoken but twenty-eight years before in the hiddenness of Carmel's cell by the unknown dying nun: "I feel that my mission is about to begin, my mission of teaching souls my Little Way, the Little Way of Spiritual Childhood".

That afternoon the Holy Father spoke for the space of an hour to the Cardinal Archbishop of Philadelphia on the subject of "his first saint", and confessed to him that never in his life had he felt so happy as he felt that day in the wonderful glorification of the little Saint "whom you in America call the Little Flower, but whom I call my guiding star".

That night the streets were thronged with pilgrims as well as with the Roman people, watching a spectacle that had not been revived since 1870.

The gigantic cupola, the Basilica façade, and even the double colonnade of the great square of St Peter's were illuminated by thousands of torches which marked out their architecture in lines of light, throwing the reflection far away, even over the distant waters of the Tiber.

"God's glory, that is my only ambition. My own I abandon to Him". So she had written in the hiddenness of Carmel. Out of that hiddenness the Heavenly Father that day lifted her with a triumph quite unique in the history of the Church, so that, through her, souls in their thousands might be drawn to love Him as she did, whose one aim had ever been "to love Jesus and to make Him loved".

The day following, the Holy Father gave a special audience to the pilgrims from France. "Few saints", he said to them, "have been God's privileged ones to the same degree as your dear little Saint. Let your lives be your thanksgiving to her who from the cloister offers us an example of perfection that everyone can and should imitate. She desires to draw us along her Little Way. Her Little Way is beautiful, fruitful, and safe. It is a way of peace and holiness, a new omen to the world, *omen novum*". The Holy Father concluded by saying that her feast would never be forgotten, for "even this Eternal City is not accustomed to such wonders".

Rome had exalted Thérèse with, to use the Holy Father's own words, "a hurricane of glory". This now spread throughout the whole world. It would be impossible to describe the magnificence of the solemnities with which the Saint was hailed in every capital in Europe and in the New World. Every church and mission throughout Asia, Africa, and India vied with one another to give expression to the greatness of their joy at the glory of one they had grown to love so much. One town alone we will mention, Lisieux, the Saint's own home.

Here the celebrations were held, on 30th September the anniversary of her death, in the Carmel she had so dearly loved. The Holy Father sent, as his Legate, Cardinal Vico, who, kneeling before the shrine, placed in the hand of the statue representing the Saint in her last sleep the golden rose which had been specially blessed by the Holy Father for that purpose. The solemnities ended with a procession in which the relics of the Saint were carried through the town, along the streets through which she had so often passed. On their way they rested for a moment in the garden of the Benedictine Convent, at the foot of the statue of Our Lady, before which St Thérèse, as a little schoolgirl, made the consecration of herself to her heavenly Mother on the day of her First Communion.

That was in 1925, and still she showers her favours on souls throughout the world. Her miracles do not cease. And thousands today make their way into the Church, won by the simplicity of her love. To her Pope Pius XI entrusted all his cares. It was this little Saint with whom he chose to confront the greatest menace of the time, for he specially placed the conversion of Russia under the shadow of her protection. So her work goes on unceasingly and will go on until the end of Time.

Proclaimed Doctor of the Church

On Sunday 19th October 1997 Pope John Paul II proclaimed Thérèse a Doctor of the Church, and during his homily at the Mass at St Peter's that day explained:

"Thérèse Martin, a discalced Carmelite of Lisieux, ardently desired to be a missionary. She was one, to the point the she could be proclaimed patroness of the missions. Jesus himself showed her how she could live this vocation: by fully practicing the commandment of love, she would be immersed in the very heart of the Church's mission, supporting those who proclaim the Gospel with the mysterious power of prayer and communion. Thus she achieved what the Second Vatican Council emphasised in teaching that the Church is missionary by nature (*cf. Ad gentes, n. 2*). Not only those who choose the missionary life but all the baptised are in some way sent *ad gentes*. This is why I chose this Missionary Sunday to proclaim St Thérèse of the Child Jesus and the Holy Face a Doctor of the universal Church: a woman, a young person, a contemplative.

Everyone thus realises that today something surprising is happening. St Thérèse of Lisieux was unable to attend a university or engage in systematic study. She died young: nevertheless, from this day forward she will be honored as a Doctor of the Church, an outstanding recognition which raises her in the esteem of the entire Christian community far beyond any academic title. Indeed, when the Magisterium proclaims someone a Doctor of the Church, it intends to point out to all the faithful, particularly to those who perform in the Church the fundamental service of preaching or who undertake the delicate task of theological teaching and research, that the doctrine professed and proclaimed by a certain person can be a reference point, not only because it conforms to revealed truth, but also because it sheds new light on the mysteries of the faith, a deeper understanding of Christ's mystery. The Council reminded us that, with the help of the Holy Spirit, understanding of the '*depositum fidei*' continually grows in the Church, and not only does the richly contemplative study to which theologians are called, not only does the Magisterium of pastors, endowed with the 'sure charism of truth', contribute to this growth process, but also that "profound understanding of spiritual things" which is given through experience, with the wealth and diversity of gifts, to all those who let themselves be docilely led by God's Spirit (cf. *Dei Verbum*, n. 8). *Lumen gentium*, for its part, teaches that God himself "speaks to us" (n. 50) in his saints. It is for this reason that the spiritual experience of the saints has a special value for deepening our knowledge of the divine mysteries, which remain ever greater than our thoughts, and not by chance does the Church choose only saints to be distinguished with the title of "Doctor". St Thérèse intensely lived the truth of love.

Thérèse of the Child Jesus and the Holy Face is the youngest of all the "Doctors of the Church", but her ardent spiritual journey shows such maturity, and the insights of faith expressed in her writings are so vast and profound that they deserve a place among the great spiritual masters. In the Apostolic Letter which I wrote for this occasion, I stressed several salient aspects of her doctrine. But how can we fail to recall here what can be considered its high point, starting with the account of the moving discovery of her special vocation in the Church? "Charity", she wrote, "gave me the key to my vocation. I understood that if the Church had a body composed of different members, the most necessary and most noble of all could not be lacking to it, and so I understood that the Church had a heart and that this heart was burning with love. I understood that it was love alone that made the Church's members act, that if love were ever extinguished, apostles would not proclaim the Gospel and martyrs would refuse to shed their blood. I understood that love includes all vocation... Then in the excess of my delirious joy, I cried out: 'O Jesus, my Love ... at last I have found my vocation; my vocation is Love!'" (Ms B, 3v). This is a wonderful passage which suffices itself to show that one can apply to St Thérèse the Gospel passage we heard in the Liturgy of the Word: "I thank you Father, Lord of heaven and earth, that you have hidden these things from the wise and understanding and revealed them to babes" (*Mt* 11:25).

Thérèse of Lisieux did not only grasp and describe the profound truth of Love as the center and heart of the Church, but in her short life she lived it intensely. It is precisely this convergence of doctrine and concrete experience, of truth and life, of teaching and practice, which shines with particular brightness in this saint, and which makes her an attractive model especially for young people and for those who are seeking true meaning for their life. Before the emptiness of so many words, Thérèse offers another solution, the one Word of salvation which, understood and lived in silence, becomes a source of renewed life. She counters a rational culture, so often overcome by practical materialism, with the disarming simplicity of the "little way" which, by returning to the essentials, leads to the secret of all life: the divine Love that surrounds and penetrates every human venture. In a time like ours, so frequently marked by an ephemeral and hedonistic culture, this new Doctor of the Church proves to be remarkably effective in enlightening the mind and heart of those who hunger and thirst for truth and love. An eminent model and guide for Christians today.

St Thérèse is present as a Doctor of the Church on the day we are celebrating World Mission Sunday. She had the ardent desire to dedicate herself to proclaiming the Gospel, and she would have liked to have crowned her witness with the supreme sacrifice of martyrdom (cf. *Ms* B, 3r). Moreover, her intense personal commitment supporting the apostolic work of Fr Maurice Bellière and Fr Adolphe Rulland, missionaries respectively in Africa and China, is well-known. In her zealous love for evangelisation, Thérèse had one ideal, as she herself says: "What we ask of him is to work for his glory, to love him and to make him loved" (*Letter* 220). The way she took to reach this ideal of life is not that of the great undertakings reserved for the few, but on the contrary, a way within everyone's reach, the "little way", a path of trust and total self-abandonment to the Lord's grace. It is not a prosaic way, as if it were less demanding. It is in fact a demanding reality, as the Gospel always is. But it is a way in which one is imbued with a sense of trusting abandonment to divine mercy, which makes even the most rigorous spiritual commitment light. Because of this way in which she receives everything as "grace", because she puts her relationship with Christ and her choice of love at the center of everything, because of the place she gives to the ardent impulses of the heart on her spiritual journey, Thérèse of Lisieux is a saint who remains young despite the passing years, and she is held up as an eminent model and guide on the path of Christians, as we approach the third millennium."

Epilogue

What is the secret of this incredible blaze of glory? It is her littleness and her simplicity. It is just this simplicity which makes so many good people fail to understand the Saint. One day a priest said to Pope Pius X that there was nothing extraordinary in the life of Thérèse. Pius X replied: "What is most extraordinary about this soul is precisely her extreme simplicity. Consult your theology". This theological truth, that sanctity lies in simplicity, is precisely the teaching most needed in our time. We men and women of the world think ourselves great, independent, self-reliant, and clever. We are complex to a degree. We cannot be simple, humble, and dependent, and so God cannot use us as He wishes. It was upon the littleness of St Thérèse, that is to say upon her consciousness of her utter nothingness apart from her Heavenly Father, her complete dependence as of a little child, and with it that confidence which only a little child can possess, it was upon these foundations that God fashioned His Saint. It is upon these foundations alone that God can build true greatness.

Our Blessed Lord humbled Himself unto death, even the death of the Cross, therefore God has exalted Him, so that at the Name of Jesus every knee shall bow.

Our Blessed Lady, because she was so humble, became the Mother of God and is now Queen of Heaven.

Little Thérèse, hidden and humbled in her nothingness in Carmel, is now held up to us by the Church as one of the greatest in the Kingdom of Heaven. Today the Catholic Church comes to us, holding Thérèse up for our example, and saying to us all: "Whosoever shall humble himself as this little child, the same is greater in the Kingdom of Heaven."

From the Apostolic Letter Proclaiming
Thérèse a Doctor of the Church

"Meeting the wishes of a great number of Brothers in the Episcopacy and very many faithful from throughout the world, having heard the opinion of the Congregation for the Causes of Saints and obtained the vote of the Congregation for the Doctrine of the Faith in what regards the eminent doctrine, with certain knowledge and mature deliberation, by the power of full apostolic authority, we declare Saint Thérèse of the Child Jesus and the Holy Face, virgin, Doctor of the Universal Church. In the name of the Father and of the Son and of the Holy Spirit."